THE STARTLED HEART

THE STARTLED HEART

Ghazal Variations on Loss

by

Eve Joseph

OOLICHAN BOOKS
LANTZVILLE, BRITISH COLUMBIA, CANADA
2004

National Library of Canada Cataloguing in Publication

Joseph, Eve, 1953-

    The startled heart / Eve Joseph.

Poems.

ISBN 0-88982-191-7

    I. Title.

PS8619.O84S73 2004   C811'.6   C2004-900888-9

Le Conseil des Arts du Canada | The Canada Council for the Arts

We gratefully acknowledge the support of the Canada Council for the Arts for our publishing program.

BRITISH COLUMBIA ARTS COUNCIL
Supported by the Province of British Columbia

Grateful acknowledgement is also made to the BC Ministry of Tourism, Small Business and Culture for their financial support.

We acknowledge the financial support of the Government of Canada through the Book Publishing Industry Development Program for our publishing activities.

Cover photograph by Marijke Friesen.

Published by
Oolichan Books
P.O. Box 10, Lantzville
British Columbia, Canada
V0R 2H0

Printed in Canada

for Duna

Foreword

There are many influences that coalesce in the writing of a poem; if we're lucky something opens in us and language breaks through in ways we had not anticipated. For me, it was the ghazal that threw open the gate and let everything in. At the heart of this form is a lightness, a touch that barely settles before it moves on. It was this quick touch that allowed me to write of loss without the full weight of sorrow. Recent dead appeared alongside old ghosts; last breaths became indistinguishable from lost songs and details surfaced from long ago encounters with those I loved. The poems are variations in that they do not adhere strictly to the tenets of the form but move according to its inherent spirit. The ghazal induces reverie and yet argues against the revered. It provides a way to hold the spiritual and the physical in the same realm: to see the light as it's leaving.

My soul is damaged like the lungs of a diamond cutter.
Beautiful and hard are the days of my life.

—Yehuda Amichai

THE STARTLED HEART

In the hour before snow, white is a kind of forgetting,
headstones and a picket fence. Who is leaving?

The way I forget, each time, how the end
is there, already, in the beginning of things.

What is lost stays lost:
one ingredient nobody remembers.

Handwriting on the recipe card,
a taste the dead take with them.

The silence of dread, sound sucked dry,
the indrawn breath. The startled heart—
a hand on the last beat. Speak now of abandonment.
Water lilies frozen on an icy pond. Small, cupped palms.

(Handwritten annotations:)
invokes personal tone.

metaphysical

personification death · em dash.

alliteration "s"

sentence fragments

transition life → death

paradox. incongruent

Concrete imagery to represent death.

talk about:
- metaphor
- punctuation / line breaks.
- paradox.
- incongruence.
- abstract vs concrete.
- juxtaposition

II

After thirty years my brother's headstone.
Someone has mowed the graveyard:

under the grass I find him:
the name *Strange* cut in stone.

A green bench streaked with birdshit:
here, our mother sits.

Sunday morning. The smell of miniature
white bells: a distant knelling.

A hand reaches for a crystal glass;
the foundation begins to shatter.

Something always about to happen:
the world before the call.

III

One death speaks to another. Late at night
a kitchen light burning. A door slightly ajar.

The dead wait patiently in hallways,
outside the window a child hovers.

At dawn, one red geranium the colour
of frank blood behind the bathroom door.

Tell me how to break through. Each time she moved
a rib cracked. Bone by bone until she flew,

surprised at the weight of wings. The way she cut air
the sweep and dip of her. A fine blade.

That was years ago. This is now:
they come holding hands, the dead

just beyond the iris on the dresser.
The way the man, dying of leukemia, said:

Death has been here three nights
and tonight I think we'll sleep together.

IV

All night music in the blue cadillac.
A river frightened you.

Blinded by faith. A second coming
until the corn stalks moved

and you were animal in the tall grass.
Fox. Coyote. A white jackrabbit

exploding out of the snow. A fire
set with twigs, hot tea. Aim high:

thirty sparrows dead at your feet.
Death so slender the palm remembers.

It was early. You heard their song.
The gospel of birds. That evangelical dawn.

V

Steady rain all night long.
Nobody sleeps in your old room.

A foot stamping outside the door.
A hand poised to knock. How hard

you have tried to keep out the cold.
My brave, brave boy. You are learning

how absence feels like love, surprised
at the comfort you find there.

First memories. Dreams.
Unsolicited and barely trustworthy.

Tell me, what is it we'll know
when the rain comes slanting home?

VI

5:00 a.m. The light tap
at the window nearly human.

A quick lick of wind. A flash
of yellow on the blackbird's wing.

Imagine the pale tenacity of the unseen guest.
Imagine death as a kind of ecology:

an air of last breaths. The living
breathing in what the dying can no longer hold.

The woman's breath was marigold.
Fetid water. Spiders came and went.

I will leave before my time.
Do not ask how I know this.

VII

All over the map. There are rivers
without water. Streets with no houses.

2:00 p.m. At last, the mailman.
What is it I so eagerly await?

Wind is never just wind,
the way grief is never just grief.

At his kitchen table, the man who digs graves
sips hot tea before he begins.

First light. Heaven cracks open.
What of the inconsolable dead?

Those accidental ghosts, the ones
for whom death has lost all interest.

Curl into the pain, the way
a drowning sailor turns into the wind.

VIII

We love, most, the ones that haunt us:
grandfather, brother. Those others

I swore never to forget. Leave me alone.
I am tired of being death's confidante.

Clothes in a heap outside the bedroom door,
what to do about the skin? What.

There are rules: how to build a fire, how to cook
for spirits. How to sing the dead to sleep.

Lizard. Tortoise. Snake. Sooner or later
we all breathe from our reptilian brain.

Anchor yourself to the living. Tie her ankle
with fine silver thread. Start now.

IX

I distrust the simplicity of belief:
the world reduced to goodness.

Where is the man they knew
as father? Vanished into prayer.

Valery feared the innocence of snow:
that call to sleep. Rest now. Rest.

Aubade. A bird
singing in the sliver of dawn.

Hymns behind the glass door.
A flicker of doubt.

Enough. First light.
He is so small now. So small.

X

You search for what is lost
with a particular blindness.

Fool. Poor mad fool.
You see her everywhere.

Crimson nails and ebony eyes:
Snow White in a Red Cross bed.

Day three without sleep, the cat
follows you from room to room.

What was the first thing you lost?
And the last?

Let her write the eulogy,
after all, it was her death.

XI

Threnody. Thin melody.
The halls of grief strangely silent.

Parallel worlds. Why is the earth
not littered with the bodies of birds?

Shadows and echoes. Those tricks.
A cormorant unfolds its slow, wet wings.

She grew up on the moors, now
she lives on the ocean's killing ground.

Wigwam Inn. 1961. The headwaters boiled
with the flashing bodies of steelhead.

Glorious suicides. Each birthday, I'm sure,
will be her last. Bloody crows.

XII

The boy made a space for himself
in his father's last days.

A great blue heron flew low
over the house. A sign? A sigh.

Not death he feared, but a final judgement:
The ones I loved I failed and would again.

What is there to say? When the breathing's erratic,
you, too, will hold your breath.

What did you expect: a blessing?
White tulips? A beholden child?

Sometimes all you can do is kneel before
the one dying. Not prayer. Another supplication.

Last wish: to live
the dying his whole life had been.

XIII

Absence defines us.
February 6th. Snow falls from a clear blue sky.

In the morning, a world so pure
it resembles nothing.

Your leaving claimed me. I became
your staunchest defender.

Wind sculpts stone in its own image:
fine-boned. A bowl to hold water.

Every time I made you up, I stood
as high as your silver belt buckle.

By moonlight: a white rainbow
and the silhouettes of mute swans.

He left when the boat outgrew
the basement. I swear it's true.

XIV

In the darkened room, grief
tiptoes around itself.

All my angels are uncertain;
they wait for me to begin.

Albino crow. Sad, strange bird.
The moon bled out tonight;

even you could think of nothing to do.
The fields hemorrhaged pale light.

Where are the wailers? The practitioners of loss?
Tonight I need my cry torn from me.

XV

With each rain, the river
takes a piece of the graveyard.

The old songs drift down the Cheakamus,
an oar poised above black water.

Poor Rose: the spirits whisper
obscenities in her ear.

White candles, cedar boughs,
and those Madonnas from Walmart.

A word for spirit, where it lives:
high in the belly, below the ribs.

Belief has backed us in a corner:
Don't eat outside after 3:00 p.m.,

be careful the name you give a child—
it may belong to someone else.

Unflinching eye. Outside her window
the owl never blinks.

In the boneyard they know each song:
the name of each singer.

XVI

After the first death:
days white as lilies.

What is more tender than the voice
bearing bad news?

I see you in a ditch.
There are no stars: no cities.

No more casual encounters,
I read you everywhere:

in the smell of smoke, in the thin blue
tongue of a hummingbird.

January. Three snowgeese winter
in the Cowichan valley: all of us earthbound.

I pray awkwardly, so far
from the child I used to be.

XVII

How will you know me in that other place?
You'll read me blind.

Rename the house wren: cactus,
canyon, marsh: a monk's disciple.

Here are the dead, without
the weight of history. Curious onlookers.

In the garden, green and white bees
disguised as snowdrops.

With each new threat,
the old deaths crowd around.

Open your eyes: there are birds
in the plum tree; one eats

from your palm. You'll know me.
You won't.

There is more: a lover.
The cry of an animal about to die.

XVIII

Drawn to the inlet, the estuary:
the sea too much for me.

A stand of white birch
and my tenacious self-doubt.

Tell me, she said, *where will I live
when they jackhammer my street?"*

I don't know. There is no getting around this.
I don't know.

Some days, sorrow: yes, and three clay birds,
frost on their delicate beaks.

I have seen bluebirds
fly from the sea. In the body

of an albatross: an angel,
heavy and slow. Things not as they seem:

a voice on the answering machine
and her, five months dead.

XIX

Think of the crow, and night.
A place to disappear. The ragged edge

of daybreak. My friend has stopped
drinking. A bird in his mouth.

A momentary collapse and the ancient ones
appear. Not human, not animal either.

You're no rook, old world bird.
You can't fool me.

A garden of snow. He is learning
a new language. Two dead mice;

the space between the indrawn breath
and the first note.

I admit, I'm surprised by the appearance
of all these birds: the leap

into nothing. Seven crows on a low sweep.
One in a tree.

At night they sleep on Senanus Island:
one black wing in the sand.

XX

Sunday morning. The Priest's robe
has native designs:

raven, eagle; a frog
with tiny human hands.

Hand to mouth to alms,
psalms and tricksters, that old song.

Late last night the fishing boats returned.
Goose moon. Next month, Loon.

What starts heavy needs to lighten:
in the kitchen sink

an ice-cream bucket of blackberries.
A permanent stain.

From his pulpit, it's that raven
proselytizing yet again.

XXI

We take with us the specifics
of memory: a slice of pear,

juice on the blade. Coved ceilings,
a garden gone to seed.

Light floods in as if he's called to it.
Not God, but the green light of trees.

A boat pulls against its anchor:
summer winds down.

In his last hours I stood by the window,
afraid to approach.

Smooth stones on the grave won't hold him:
he stays by choice.

XXII

A man draws on a woman's body:
thin blue lines. Deserted streets.

Bare trees draw the eye. Only
the intrepid winter here.

Pain moves on small feet
across her belly.

Tonight children dance in a dead man's
hats: his body laid out on the bed.

The table set. I wish for wild salmon.
A house without cancer.

The names of the dead: a grid.
My map of the city.

XXIII

Settle down. Panic, too,
is prayer. A dangerous obsession:

feeding the stars by fire,
and nobody to tell.

In the garden, a ghost, unconcerned,
works the soil.

Such beauty in the flawed: sitting down
to the evening meal. Pass the potatoes, please.

I do not see what he sees. A blank canvas:
his mind on it. A line of fire.

If a *radif*, then let it be mercy.
Singed by fear: a near miss. Dear God, mercy.

XXIV

Let's not fool ourselves,
the beautiful death promises nothing.

I can no longer tell privilege
from disaster.

A slight breeze, the window open
just after.

Comatose, she slipped into
her green silk dress.

So quiet, the turn toward
one's death. What's left?

No avatars or holy men, only a human
angel swimming toward light.

XXV

What we hold of fire
in our hands: ashes, burnt words,

a cracked plate: a boy
on the other side licking it clean.

The smell of smoke: a fistful
of lily of the valley. For you, love, for you.

The wrought iron gate keeps nobody out.
Delicate black vines and grapes.

I cook crepes for my brother,
thirty years later:

feed him in death
as I never could in life.

XXVI

for John Thompson

Someone said, look. And you did.
A homeless mind: an unrelenting eye.

Is this where we meet?
On the edge of a brief light?

I imagine the marshes: shot through
with gray. Waterfowl. An unwary sky.

You touched what was yours: words,
a great fish, the light as it left.

Fire-eater. Starboy. Heaven's gatekeeper.
So many choices for one so young.

A reverie, this madness. Impossible
to resist. Tantramar. A voice

from the abattoir.
A hunter's moon on the rise.

XXVII

I wake to a mourning
already begun. Reconfigured;

when I stop spinning
I can't say what I'll be.

The light above the porch has burned
out. Moths circle the dark glass.

March 3rd. Crocuses push past the mud;
the gravedigger hits clay, cuts past

the sleeping snakes, and the dead
stand around the terrestrial fires, listless,

warming their hands
in the slow burn toward morning.

XXVIII

A starling with no feet
eats at my table: crumbs, dried berries.

Where does it get me,
this foolish pity?

Intentional or not, you stepped
in death's way. A bone-white edge

the near perfect fit
of broken things.

It's hope that does me in: the place
the voice breaks.

Too late for lessons now. A blackbird
spoke in the break of dawn.

What's left? A kind of grace:
a perilous landing.

XXIX

Each death leads me, reluctantly,
to my own beliefs.

3:00 a.m., a ravenous fire
feeds on prayer. A constant wind.

I'm sorry, love, this first loss:
the white flight of bees.

He's scattered in the mountains,
beneath the apple tree: he's

a fistful of ashes
in a small, red boat.

Let them come, those who loved him:
call them home from the river.

Map stars by daylight. Chart
the lost valleys. A small beginning.

XXX

Against such blue skies the crow
finds nowhere to hide.

In my death poem light will find me
defiant and unprepared.

I'll write a letter to my children,
steal what I must: white fields

and a man writing himself off
to God.

How quickly we doubt
the brief glimpse. Don't

look for me in the accidental:
animal, I'll track you down.

The mind returns
to the last place, finds

the river is, after all,
only a river.

Ravens fly straight, not crows:
tell me, which way will I go?

XXXI

Imagine silence rolling in, sound
waiting to break against something.

[handwritten: paradox (line can be read more than one way?)]

Anything. I want the details:
what clothes were you buried in?

Were your feet bare? What markers
there were are overgrown.

I'll trade a stone for a solitary tree.
A long stretch of highway;

a chorus of frogs
and the stunned face of God.

Strange, I mistakenly thought the poem
could hold your broken body.

[handwritten: inibility to deal with death]

And you, shoeless, walking a dirt path
to the unwalled city.

[handwritten: light up, light up as if you have ~~choices~~. choice.]

43

XXXII

What I disturb catches my eye:
a sudden movement, then nothing.

Tell me again about the daughters of song,
the circle of delicate bones.

A singing of sorts. Notes pieced together
from a dimly lit room.

I watch a hawk hunt: the day is long.
The tide beginning to turn.

On the rooftops of Jerusalem
men walk secret pathways

and the mourners go about the streets,
slowly, in their skin of flames.

Learning to sing I stole only
what was necessary: dirt, water, cedar kindling.

XXXIII

Something grows, undetected,
in the shadow of the heart.

Once he thought his bed a skiff,
once a yellow bus with no brakes.

Those who watch do so
with the eyes of the living;

the ones who peek into heaven
do not say what they see.

Only once did I hear a bird sing
in a garden that didn't exist.

Death planed him thinner
and thinner:

held to the light,
he would surely burn.

XXXIV

Late fall, frogs announce
it is time to dance.

Are those men or ghosts
circling the fire?

I doubt what I know,
not what I hear: old songs

rise from the burnt church,
not hymns but hunting songs.

Was it madness to let her sleep
on the grave? Madness to drag her off?

Always the river, its secrets:
an osprey hooked: a terrible kite.

Her Indian bread was so fine
we called it cake.

XXXV

Fish breathing in the Daffodil Motel.
Go. Go now. Don't go.

Two bronze cranes keep
the herons away. At night

a white cat, an apparition
at the foot of the garden.

Sickness crept on all fours,
sank its claw deep in her lung.

She was loved to the last scrap
of her life. Open-mouthed,

fish out of water. A good day's catch.
An armful of yellow flowers.

Long after the last exhalation,
the heart firing, still.

XXXVI

Jarrett tonight. That grace. The dying
in their beds. Five planets lining up.

Is it order I seek, or release? The last
shallow breaths or the merciful death?

Overnight the shoreline altered:
what existed earlier is no more.

A fine rain brings the sky closer
to earth; the urge

to reach through what can't be seen.
A grace. Between notes, an exhalation.

What could these be, the unlit stars,
if not the uncut stones of heaven?

XXXVII

These were the terrible things: a crow
in the chimney, a picture falling.

On my street the Italians wore black:
old crones, wings tucked up close.

Tell me, who lets go first:
the living or the dead?

All summer long we half-expected
the river to give him back.

Move over crows. My turn to walk
the tightrope. Three steps and I'll fly.

Nothing fell the day he died:
not a pin dropped.

XXXVIII

What I neglect
creates its own disorder:

I forget to send the dead away
and they forget to leave.

You'd think one of us could
return the garden to its true beauty.

The red birdhouse is empty:
sadly, nothing winters in my backyard.

After the funeral, the last
visitor gone, the new ghosts

read their burnt letters
while the old pick through the ash

looking for nothing in particular.
The graveyard finally still.

XXXIX

I want to be anonymous,
the stranger on a narrow street:

close by, the ones I love,
oblivious and happy.

I stumble where you stopped:
this morning a bird repeats one long,

then four sharp notes; my ear
hears only the pattern, not the song.

Your poems were notes flung
from tree to tree:

hunger songs, blackout songs; songs
that repeated what you knew of loss:

of love. This is where I leave you:
in the crow's white breath,

on the branch,
after the landing.

XL

August 17th. Fall has crept in
one red leaf at a time: the Sumac

sticky with the fine silver threads
of abandoned webs.

They travel quickly, the dead:
a lamp flickers before the call.

Speak of the poem: dark water
and a man dying in a strange city:

she took in his gaunt face; slowly,
she took in the length of his spirit.

In the beginning I forget
the end is there. I'm sorry

I do not see
what she sees.

XLI

On the floodplain, in the bouldering fields,
the moon belongs to no season.

Before speech, a language
first spoken on the riverbank: a cry.

In the snow, twelve eagles
spread their wings to dry.

Cheakamus, Mamquam, Cheekye:
I can't place you on earth or sky.

Beginnings. A child molded
out of clay. A salmon scale. A seed.

Who would believe
the hungriest ghost was the baby?

XLII

What there was of silence has been
lost to the untranslatable:

wind, birds, rain. The involuntary
cries of the inconsolable.

Begin again: after hope what then?
A winter garden. Stubborn flowers.

A sparrow, luminous, on his bedside table,
as in: a new vessel, flight, release.

The window open, three inches,
just in case.

Night never fails to silence the birds;
or is darkness their most familiar song?

XLIII

We return to our childhood languages:
the small rooms of memory.

A woman singing behind a door,
a man in his garden reading aloud.

I waited for the sandman
until my eyes grew gritty with sleep.

September 20th. Plums are to be stolen,
on this we agree.

To the man this morning, I wanted
to say, *you'll drift away,* but that's a lie;

a traveller he was by then, indecipherable:
home was coming closer.

XLIV

I've stolen my own rituals: notes
are missing. Whole songs forgotten.

On my wrist, a raven feeding
on spirits. What to make of this?

A hand reached through pain
to a stone temple. A bell. A winter wren.

Wind. Breath. It seemed the whole
world waited on this death.

Around the shed, a string of unlit lanterns:
small fires in the sky.

Fear darkens the room: a candle
helps. And touch.

Today, I move against the current;
even a short crossing takes longer.

October 3rd. Grateful for the late sun:
the last, unhurried bees.

XLV

November 5th. The rivers are rising;
instinctually, we edge closer to home.

One body, they rise: drop
back to earth. To these fields.

Don't confuse me for the angel
of death. Clearly, I lack the conviction.

The dugout is all we have left: that
and a memory of fire.

Think of them as snow birds:
small, white fidelities.

What breaks through ice rises:
a song, a spirit song.

It is here I release the dead:
navigators on a starless night.

Acknowledgements

Some of these poems previously appeared in: *The Malahat Review, Event, Prism International, The Fiddlehead, Margie: The American Journal of Poetry, volumes one and two and The Globe and Mail—How Poems Work.*

I am grateful for the assistance provided by the Canada Council during the writing of these poems. My thanks to Lorna Crozier for her fine ear and editorial insight and to Susan Musgrave for including three of the ghazals in the Globe and Mail. Thanks as well to Hiro Boga, Ron Smith and the staff at Oolichan Books. And thanks to Chris Hutchinson for our ongoing conversation about poetry. My love and appreciation to my children: Leigh, Saul and Salia and to my love, Patrick.

About the Author

Eve Joseph was born in 1953 and grew up in North Vancouver. As a young woman she worked on freighters and traveled widely before moving to Vancouver Island where she now lives in Brentwood Bay. She has her M.A. in Counselling Psychology and works at Victoria Hospice.